HOUGHTON MIFFLIN HARCOURT

Daily Language Workouts

Grade 2

Interactive Whiteboard Compatible!

Daily MUG Shot Sentences
Weekly MUG Shot Paragraphs
Writing Prompts
Writing Topics
Show-Me Sentences

GREAT SOURCE®

HOUGHTON MIFFLIN HARCOURT

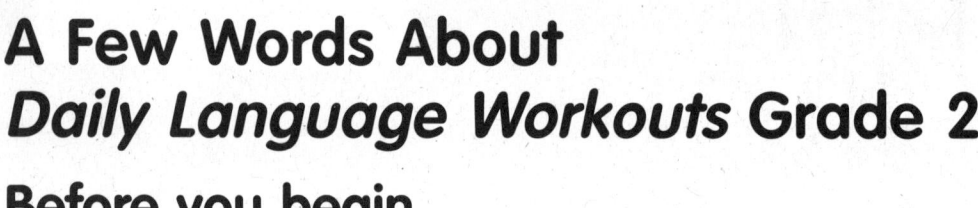

A Few Words About
Daily Language Workouts Grade 2

Before you begin . . .

The activities in this book will help your students develop basic writing and language skills. You'll find three types of exercises on the following pages:

MUG Shot Sentences There are 180 sentences highlighting **m**echanics, **u**sage, and/or **g**rammar (MUG), one for each day of the school year. For the first 27 weeks, focused sentences concentrate on one skill per week. For the final 9 weeks, sentences present a mixed review, and students are asked to correct several types of errors in each sentence.

MUG Shot Paragraphs There are 36 weekly paragraphs. The first 27 correspond directly with each week's MUG Shot sentences, focusing on the same mechanics, usage, or grammar error. The final 9 paragraphs present a mixed review of the covered proofreading and editing skills.

Daily Writing Practice This section begins with **writing prompts** that include topics and graphics designed to inspire expository, narrative, descriptive, persuasive, and creative writing. Next, a discussion of daily journal writing introduces the lists of intriguing **writing topics**. Finally, the **show-me sentences** provide starting points for paragraphs, essays, and other writing forms.

Write Source Online provides the lessons in this book for interactive whiteboard instruction. To use, open the files from *Write Source Online* using your whiteboard software.

Trademarks and trade names are shown in this book strictly for illustrative purposes and are the property of their respective owners. The authors' references herein should not be regarded as affecting their validity.

Copyright © by Houghton Mifflin Harcourt Publishing Company

All rights reserved. No part of this work may be reproduced or transmitted in any form or by any means, electronic or mechanical, including photocopying or recording, or by any information storage or retrieval system, without the prior written permission of the copyright owner unless such copying is expressly permitted by federal copyright law.

Permission is hereby granted to individuals using the corresponding student's textbook or kit as the major vehicle for regular classroom instruction to photocopy entire pages from this publication in classroom quantities for instructional use and not for resale. Requests for information on other matters regarding duplication of this work should be addressed to Houghton Mifflin Harcourt Publishing Company, Attn: Paralegal, 9400 South Park Center Loop, Orlando, Florida 32819.

Printed in the U.S.A.

ISBN 978-0-547-48512-6

1 2 3 4 5 6 7 8 9 10 11 12 0956 15 14 13 12 11 10

4500251434   A B C D E F G

If you have received these materials as examination copies free of charge, Houghton Mifflin Harcourt Publishing Company retains title to the materials and they may not be resold. Resale of examination copies is strictly prohibited.

Possession of this publication in print format does not entitle users to convert this publication, or any portion of it, into electronic format.

Table of Contents

Editing and Proofreading Marks   iv

MUG Shot Sentences

MUG Shot Sentence Organizer	**2**
Implementation and Evaluation	**3**
Focused Sentences	**4**
Mixed-Review Sentences	**58**

MUG Shot Paragraphs

Implementation and Evaluation	**78**
Focused Paragraphs	**79**
Mixed-Review Paragraphs	**106**

Daily Writing Practice

Writing Prompts	**116**
Writing Topics	**141**
Show-Me Sentences	**145**

Editing and Proofreading Marks

These symbols may be used to correct MUG Shot sentences and paragraphs.

Add a letter, a word, or words.	∧	take∧home (them)
Add a comma.	∧,	Troy∧Michigan
Add a period.	⊙	Mrs⊙
Add a question mark or an exclamation point.	?∧ !∧	How about you?∧
Capitalize a letter.	/ (or) ≡	/toronto (or) toronto≡ (T)
Make a capital letter lowercase.	/	/History (or) /History (h)
Replace or take something out.	— (or) ɣ	a hot day (or) a hot day (cold)
Add an apostrophe.	⋎'	Bill's
Add quotation marks.	⋎" ⋎"	"Wow!"
Use italics (underlining).	___	The Tiny Seed

MUG Shot Sentences

The MUG Shot sentences are designed to be used at the beginning of each class period as a quick and efficient way to review **m**echanics, **u**sage, and **g**rammar. Each sentence can be corrected and discussed in 3 to 5 minutes.

MUG Shot Sentence Organizer	2
Implementation and Evaluation	3
Focused Sentences	4
Mixed-Review Sentences	58

MUG Shot Sentence Organizer

Name _____ Date _____

Corrected Sentence:

Corrected Sentence:

Corrected Sentence:

Corrected Sentence:

Corrected Sentence:

Implementation and Evaluation

The first 27 weeks of MUG Shot sentences are focused sentences covering one proofreading skill per week. The remaining 9 weeks of MUG Shot sentences provide mixed reviews of two or three proofreading skills per sentence.

Implementation

Write the MUG Shot sentence on the board. Read it aloud to be sure students understand it. Then write the correction on the board as a volunteer provides it. If you wish, have students write the corrected form in their notebooks.

Otherwise, you may write a sentence on the board at the beginning of the class period, allowing time for students to read the sentence silently. Read the sentence aloud before actual work begins. Then have students correct the MUG Shot in their notebooks (or on a copy of the "MUG Shot Sentence Organizer," page 2 of this book). As a class, discuss the reasons for students' corrections.

Each Friday, review the week's MUG Shots. Consider assigning the corresponding MUG Shot paragraph. (See page 77.)

Evaluation

If you assign sentences daily, evaluate your students' work at the end of the week. We recommend that you give them a basic performance score based on having each sentence written correctly in their language arts notebooks.

Week 1: Focused Sentences

✱ **Period at the End of a Telling Sentence**

I like to cook with my dad

✱ **Period at the End of a Telling Sentence**

He makes the best blueberry pancakes

✱ **Period at the End of a Telling Sentence**

My job is to add the flour to the bowl

✱ **Period at the End of a Telling Sentence**

Sometimes Dad lets me break an egg

✱ **Period at the End of a Telling Sentence**

We have fun making pancake people together

Week 1: Corrected Sentences

* **Period at the End of a Telling Sentence**

    I like to cook with my dad.

* **Period at the End of a Telling Sentence**

    He makes the best blueberry pancakes.

* **Period at the End of a Telling Sentence**

    My job is to add the flour to the bowl.

* **Period at the End of a Telling Sentence**

    Sometimes Dad lets me break an egg.

* **Period at the End of a Telling Sentence**

    We have fun making pancake people together.

Week 2: Focused Sentences

* **Period After an Abbreviation**

    Our music teacher is Mrs Marino.

* **Period After an Abbreviation**

    Mom took Ben to see Dr Khan.

* **Period After an Abbreviation**

    Mrs Beasley is a kind principal.

* **Period After an Abbreviation**

    Mr Hunt lives across the street from us.

* **Period After an Abbreviation**

    Our gym teacher is Ms Ryan.

Week 2: Corrected Sentences

* **Period After an Abbreviation**

    Our music teacher is Mrs. Marino.

* **Period After an Abbreviation**

    Mom took Ben to see Dr. Khan.

* **Period After an Abbreviation**

    Mrs. Beasley is a kind principal.

* **Period After an Abbreviation**

    Mr. Hunt lives across the street from us.

* **Period After an Abbreviation**

    Our gym teacher is Ms. Ryan.

MUG Shot Sentences

Week 3: Focused Sentences

* **Period After an Initial**

    My name is Ruthie J Allan.

* **Period After an Initial**

    H A Rey wrote the book Curious George.

* **Period After an Initial**

    My friend's nickname is T J.

* **Period After an Initial**

    John D MacArthur Beach State Park is in Florida.

* **Period After an Initial**

    The inventor, J L Love, invented the pencil sharpener.

Week 3: Corrected Sentences

* **Period After an Initial**

  My name is Ruthie J. Allan.

* **Period After an Initial**

  H. A. Rey wrote the book <u>Curious George</u>.

* **Period After an Initial**

  My friend's nickname is T. J.

* **Period After an Initial**

  John D. MacArthur Beach State Park is in Florida.

* **Period After an Initial**

  The inventor, J. L. Love, invented the pencil sharpener.

Week 4: Focused Sentences

* **Question Mark After a Question**

    How many continents are there

* **Question Mark After a Question**

    What is the biggest lake in this country

* **Question Mark After a Question**

    When will the United States be 300 years old

* **Question Mark After a Question**

    Are nickels bigger than dimes

* **Question Mark After a Question**

    Who wrote Little House in the Big Woods

Week 4: Corrected Sentences

* **Question Mark After a Question**

    How many continents are there?

* **Question Mark After a Question**

    What is the biggest lake in this country?

* **Question Mark After a Question**

    When will the United States be 300 years old?

* **Question Mark After a Question**

    Are nickels bigger than dimes?

* **Question Mark After a Question**

    Who wrote <u>Little House in the Big Woods</u>?

MUG Shot Sentences

Week 5: Focused Sentences

* **Exclamation Point After a Sentence That Shows Strong Feeling**

  Look at that catch

* **Exclamation Point After a Sentence That Shows Strong Feeling**

  The left fielder crashed into the wall

* **Exclamation Point After a Sentence That Shows Strong Feeling**

  The bases are loaded

* **Exclamation Point After a Sentence That Shows Strong Feeling**

  Amazing Austin will save the day

* **Exclamation Point After a Sentence That Shows Strong Feeling**

  Oh no, he struck out

Week 5: Corrected Sentences

* **Exclamation Point After a Sentence That Shows Strong Feeling**

  Look at that catch!

* **Exclamation Point After a Sentence That Shows Strong Feeling**

  The left fielder crashed into the wall!

* **Exclamation Point After a Sentence That Shows Strong Feeling**

  The bases are loaded!

* **Exclamation Point After a Sentence That Shows Strong Feeling**

  Amazing Austin will save the day!

* **Exclamation Point After a Sentence That Shows Strong Feeling**

  Oh no, he struck out!

Week 6: Focused Sentences

* **Capital Letter for the First Word in a Sentence**

  our read-aloud book is called <u>The Chalk Box Kid</u>.

* **Capital Letter for the First Word in a Sentence**

  i love getting letters in the mail.

* **Capital Letter for the First Word in a Sentence**

  "do you like to swim in the ocean?" he asked.

* **Capital Letter for the First Word in a Sentence**

  mrs. Lambert is my favorite neighbor.

* **Capital Letter for the First Word in a Sentence**

  the highest mountain I've seen is in Alaska.

Week 6: Corrected Sentences

* **Capital Letter for the First Word in a Sentence**

    O
    ø̸ur read-aloud book is called <u>The Chalk Box Kid</u>.

* **Capital Letter for the First Word in a Sentence**

    I
    i̸ love getting letters in the mail.

* **Capital Letter for the First Word in a Sentence**

    D
    "d̸o you like to swim in the ocean?" he asked.

* **Capital Letter for the First Word in a Sentence**

    M
    m̸rs. Lambert is my favorite neighbor.

* **Capital Letter for the First Word in a Sentence**

    T
    t̸he highest mountain I've seen is in Alaska.

Week 7: Focused Sentences

* **Capital Letter for the Word *I***

  One thing i enjoy is collecting seashells.

* **Capital Letter for the Word *I***

  i like the scallops, tulips, and buttercups.

* **Capital Letter for the Word *I***

  It's important to use sunscreen when i go shelling.

* **Capital Letter for the Word *I***

  Sometimes i find shells buried in the sand.

* **Capital Letter for the Word *I***

  Once i found a big sea biscuit while snorkeling.

Week 7: Corrected Sentences

* **Capital Letter for the Word I**

  One thing ̷i enjoy is collecting seashells.

* **Capital Letter for the Word I**

  ̷i like the scallops, tulips, and buttercups.

* **Capital Letter for the Word I**

  It's important to use sunscreen when ̷i go shelling.

* **Capital Letter for the Word I**

  Sometimes ̷i find shells buried in the sand.

* **Capital Letter for the Word I**

  Once ̷i found a big sea biscuit while snorkeling.

MUG Shot Sentences

Week 8: Focused Sentences

* **Capital Letters for Days, Months, and Holidays**

   We had a valentine's day party in february.

* **Capital Letters for Days, Months, and Holidays**

   Memorial day is always on a monday.

* **Capital Letters for Days, Months, and Holidays**

   We will do our book reports on wednesday.

* **Capital Letters for Days, Months, and Holidays**

   In june we will have a storybook parade!

* **Capital Letters for Days, Months, and Holidays**

   Next september we will be in third grade!

MUG Shot Sentences

Week 8: Corrected Sentences

* **Capital Letters for Days, Months, and Holidays**

  We had a ~~v~~Valentine's ~~d~~Day party in ~~f~~February.

* **Capital Letters for Days, Months, and Holidays**

  Memorial ~~d~~Day is always on a ~~m~~Monday.

* **Capital Letters for Days, Months, and Holidays**

  We will do our book reports on ~~w~~Wednesday.

* **Capital Letters for Days, Months, and Holidays**

  In ~~j~~June we will have a storybook parade!

* **Capital Letters for Days, Months, and Holidays**

  Next ~~s~~September we will be in third grade!

MUG Shot Sentences

Week 9: Focused Sentences

✱ **Capital Letters for Names of Places**

Our family wants to visit the grand canyon.

✱ **Capital Letters for Names of Places**

The grand canyon is in arizona.

✱ **Capital Letters for Names of Places**

We'll drive through texas and new mexico.

✱ **Capital Letters for Names of Places**

I hope we will see the rio grande river.

✱ **Capital Letters for Names of Places**

We'll go through colorado on our way home.

Week 9: Corrected Sentences

* **Capital Letters for Names of Places**

    Our family wants to visit the ~~g~~Grand ~~c~~Canyon.

* **Capital Letters for Names of Places**

    The ~~g~~Grand ~~c~~Canyon is in ~~a~~Arizona.

* **Capital Letters for Names of Places**

    We'll drive through ~~t~~Texas and ~~n~~New ~~m~~Mexico.

* **Capital Letters for Names of Places**

    I hope we will see the ~~r~~Rio ~~g~~Grande ~~r~~River.

* **Capital Letters for Names of Places**

    We'll go through ~~c~~Colorado on our way home.

MUG Shot Sentences

Week 10: Focused Sentences

* **Capital Letters for Names and Titles**

    lavon raced billy joe to the playground.

* **Capital Letters for Names and Titles**

    John price and peter mann played catch.

* **Capital Letters for Names and Titles**

    We played kick ball with mr. meyer's class.

* **Capital Letters for Names and Titles**

    mrs. kelly blew her whistle three times.

* **Capital Letters for Names and Titles**

    julie called, "It's time to line up now!"

Week 10: Corrected Sentences

* **Capital Letters for Names and Titles**

  L   B J
  ~~l~~avon raced ~~b~~illy ~~j~~oe to the playground.

* **Capital Letters for Names and Titles**

          P   P   M
  John ~~p~~rice and ~~p~~eter ~~m~~ann played catch.

* **Capital Letters for Names and Titles**

                            M M
  We played kick ball with ~~m~~r. ~~m~~eyer's class.

* **Capital Letters for Names and Titles**

  M   K
  ~~m~~rs. ~~k~~elly blew her whistle three times.

* **Capital Letters for Names and Titles**

  J
  ~~j~~ulie called, "It's time to line up now!"

Week 11: Focused Sentences

* **Plurals That Add -s**

  Megan made a picnic lunch for her three sister.

* **Plurals That Add -es**

  Sydney ate bunchs of grapes.

* **Plurals That Add -es**

  Alexis liked the peanut butter sandwichs.

* **Plurals That Add -s**

  Marissa drank two carton of milk.

* **Plurals That Add -es**

  The girls were happy with their lunchs.

Week 11: Corrected Sentences

* **Plurals That Add -s**

   Megan made a picnic lunch for her three ~~sister~~ sisters.

* **Plurals That Add -es**

   Sydney ate ~~bunchs~~ bunches of grapes.

* **Plurals That Add -es**

   Alexis liked the peanut butter ~~sandwichs~~ sandwiches.

* **Plurals That Add -s**

   Marissa drank two ~~carton~~ cartons of milk.

* **Plurals That Add -es**

   The girls were happy with their ~~lunchs~~ lunches.

Week 12: Focused Sentences

* **Using the Right Word**

  Did you here that train whistle?

* **Using the Right Word**

  The train goes by at for o'clock each day.

* **Using the Right Word**

  Susan saw the train this time, but eye didn't.

* **Using the Right Word**

  I wonder wear it is going today.

* **Using the Right Word**

  Johnny wood like to be a conductor someday.

Week 12: Corrected Sentences

* **Using the Right Word**

  Did you ~~here~~ hear that train whistle?

* **Using the Right Word**

  The train goes by at ~~for~~ four o'clock each day.

* **Using the Right Word**

  Susan saw the train this time, but ~~eye~~ I didn't.

* **Using the Right Word**

  I wonder ~~wear~~ where it is going today.

* **Using the Right Word**

  Johnny ~~wood~~ would like to be a conductor someday.

MUG Shot Sentences

Week 13: Focused Sentences

* **Comma Between a City and a State**

    Dennis lives in Dennisville New Jersey.

* **Comma Between a City and a State**

    Annie can't wait to go to San Antonio Texas.

* **Comma Between a City and a State**

    Milford Michigan, is where Katie lives.

* **Comma Between a City and a State**

    Would you like to visit Friendly West Virginia?

* **Comma Between a City and a State**

    Do many writers live in Pencil Bluff Arkansas?

Week 13: Corrected Sentences

* **Comma Between a City and a State**

    Dennis lives in Dennisville, New Jersey.

* **Comma Between a City and a State**

    Annie can't wait to go to San Antonio, Texas.

* **Comma Between a City and a State**

    Milford, Michigan, is where Katie lives.

* **Comma Between a City and a State**

    Would you like to visit Friendly, West Virginia?

* **Comma Between a City and a State**

    Do many writers live in Pencil Bluff, Arkansas?

Week 14: Focused Sentences

* **Comma Between the Day and the Year**

    My brother was born on March 15 2004.

* **Comma Between the Day and the Year**

    Our family went on vacation on June 15 2010.

* **Comma Between the Day and the Year**

    On July 4 2001, the United States was 225 years old.

* **Comma Between the Day and the Year**

    On March 21 2005, Regan was 10 years old.

* **Comma Between the Day and the Year**

    She turned 11 years old on February 27 2010.

Week 14: Corrected Sentences

* **Comma Between the Day and the Year**

    My brother was born on March 15, 2004.

* **Comma Between the Day and the Year**

    Our family went on vacation on June 15, 2010.

* **Comma Between the Day and the Year**

    On July 4, 2001, the United States was 225 years old.

* **Comma Between the Day and the Year**

    On March 21, 2005, Regan was 10 years old.

* **Comma Between the Day and the Year**

    She turned 11 years old on February 27, 2010.

Week 15: Focused Sentences

✱ **Comma After the Greeting and the Closing in a Letter**

Dear Aunt Mya

    Thank you for my new sweater. The stripes are cool. I wore it to school today.

                    Love

                    Ben

✱ **Comma After the Greeting and the Closing in a Letter**

Dear Grandma Diane

    Will you come to my tea party? It's on Saturday at 11:00. I will serve sesame-seed crackers. I hope you can come!

                    Your granddaughter

                    Kathryn

Week 15: Corrected Sentences

✱ Comma After the Greeting and the Closing in a Letter

Dear Aunt Mya,

    Thank you for my new sweater. The stripes are cool. I wore it to school today.

                      Love,
                        Ben

✱ Comma After the Greeting and the Closing in a Letter

Dear Grandma Diane,

    Will you come to my tea party? It's on Saturday at 11:00. I will serve sesame-seed crackers. I hope you can come!

                      Your granddaughter,
                      Kathryn

Week 16: Focused Sentences

✶ **Using the Right Word**

Our cousins came to sea us at Thanksgiving.

✶ **Using the Right Word**

Mom served to kinds of meat for dinner.

✶ **Using the Right Word**

Ant Janie read us some stories after dessert.

✶ **Using the Right Word**

I love the one about the son and the wind.

✶ **Using the Right Word**

Grandma blue kisses to everyone.

Week 16: Corrected Sentences

* **Using the Right Word**

    Our cousins came to ~~sea~~ *see* us at Thanksgiving.

* **Using the Right Word**

    Mom served ~~to~~ *two* kinds of meat for dinner.

* **Using the Right Word**

    ~~Ant~~ *Aunt* Janie read us some stories after dessert.

* **Using the Right Word**

    I love the one about the ~~son~~ *sun* and the wind.

* **Using the Right Word**

    Grandma ~~blue~~ *blew* kisses to everyone.

Week 17: Focused Sentences

* **Apostrophe to Make a Contraction**

  Mr. Wallace hasnt checked our tests yet.

* **Apostrophe to Make a Contraction**

  I dont think I made any mistakes.

* **Apostrophe to Make a Contraction**

  Well get our spelling tests back after lunch.

* **Apostrophe to Make a Contraction**

  Maria cant find her spelling book.

* **Apostrophe to Make a Contraction**

  She wasnt sure how to spell "house."

Week 17: Corrected Sentences

* **Apostrophe to Make a Contraction**

  Mr. Wallace hasn't checked our tests yet.

* **Apostrophe to Make a Contraction**

  I don't think I made any mistakes.

* **Apostrophe to Make a Contraction**

  We'll get our spelling tests back after lunch.

* **Apostrophe to Make a Contraction**

  Maria can't find her spelling book.

* **Apostrophe to Make a Contraction**

  She wasn't sure how to spell "house."

Week 18: Focused Sentences

* **Apostrophe to Show Ownership**

    My familys favorite drive-in sells sub sandwiches.

* **Apostrophe to Show Ownership**

    Sliced turkey is Jannas favorite.

* **Apostrophe to Show Ownership**

    Moms hot meatball sandwich is really messy.

* **Apostrophe to Show Ownership**

    My sisters favorite sandwich is ham and cheese.

* **Apostrophe to Show Ownership**

    I always taste Dads hot tea.

Week 18: Corrected Sentences

* **Apostrophe to Show Ownership**

  My family's favorite drive-in sells sub sandwiches.

* **Apostrophe to Show Ownership**

  Sliced turkey is Janna's favorite.

* **Apostrophe to Show Ownership**

  Mom's hot meatball sandwich is really messy.

* **Apostrophe to Show Ownership**

  My sister's favorite sandwich is ham and cheese.

* **Apostrophe to Show Ownership**

  I always taste Dad's hot tea.

MUG Shot Sentences

Week 19: Focused Sentences

* **Irregular Plurals**

    All of the childs learned about fire safety.

* **Irregular Plurals**

    Zachary told storys around the campfire.

* **Irregular Plurals**

    P. J. lost two tooths last weekend.

* **Irregular Plurals**

    Oh no! Mouses got into our picnic basket.

* **Irregular Plurals**

    We saw sheeps on our drive through the country.

Week 19: Corrected Sentences

* **Irregular Plurals**

    All of the ~~childs~~ *children* learned about fire safety.

* **Irregular Plurals**

    Zachary told ~~storys~~ *stories* around the campfire.

* **Irregular Plurals**

    P. J. lost two ~~tooths~~ *teeth* last weekend.

* **Irregular Plurals**

    Oh no! ~~Mouses~~ *Mice* got into our picnic basket.

* **Irregular Plurals**

    We saw ~~sheeps~~ *sheep* on our drive through the country.

Week 20: Focused Sentences

* **Comma Between Words in a Series**

    Wyoming Utah and Idaho are western states.

* **Comma Between Words in a Series**

    Hawaii is warm sunny and beautiful.

* **Comma Between Words in a Series**

    I can swim skate and fish in Minnesota.

* **Comma Between Words in a Series**

    Florida Alabama and Georgia are in the South.

* **Comma Between Words in a Series**

    Cherries apples and peaches grow in Michigan.

Week 20: Corrected Sentences

* **Comma Between Words in a Series**

    Wyoming, Utah, and Idaho are western states.

* **Comma Between Words in a Series**

    Hawaii is warm, sunny, and beautiful.

* **Comma Between Words in a Series**

    I can swim, skate, and fish in Minnesota.

* **Comma Between Words in a Series**

    Florida, Alabama, and Georgia are in the South.

* **Comma Between Words in a Series**

    Cherries, apples, and peaches grow in Michigan.

Week 21: Focused Sentences

* **Comma in a Compound Sentence**

    My brother loves football but I like baseball.

* **Comma in a Compound Sentence**

    Do you want the black checkers or do you want the red ones?

* **Comma in a Compound Sentence**

    I got a new pet iguana and I named him Rex.

* **Comma in a Compound Sentence**

    I went to Ashanti's house but she was not home.

* **Comma in a Compound Sentence**

    We can eat out or we can order pizza.

Week 21: Corrected Sentences

* **Comma in a Compound Sentence**

    My brother loves football, but I like baseball.

* **Comma in a Compound Sentence**

    Do you want the black checkers, or do you want the red ones?

* **Comma in a Compound Sentence**

    I got a new pet iguana, and I named him Rex.

* **Comma in a Compound Sentence**

    I went to Ashanti's house, but she was not home.

* **Comma in a Compound Sentence**

    We can eat out, or we can order pizza.

Week 22: Focused Sentences

* **Comma to Help Set Off a Speaker's Words**

  Mrs. Frazzle called "It's time for gym!"

* **Comma to Help Set Off a Speaker's Words**

  "After gym, we can have a treat" said Mike.

* **Comma to Help Set Off a Speaker's Words**

  Joshua asked "What treat did you bring?"

* **Comma to Help Set Off a Speaker's Words**

  "It's a surprise" Michael answered.

* **Comma to Help Set Off a Speaker's Words**

  Shana whispered "I can't wait to find out!"

Week 22: Corrected Sentences

* **Comma to Help Set Off a Speaker's Words**

   Mrs. Frazzle called, "It's time for gym!"

* **Comma to Help Set Off a Speaker's Words**

   "After gym, we can have a treat," said Mike.

* **Comma to Help Set Off a Speaker's Words**

   Joshua asked, "What treat did you bring?"

* **Comma to Help Set Off a Speaker's Words**

   "It's a surprise," Michael answered.

* **Comma to Help Set Off a Speaker's Words**

   Shana whispered, "I can't wait to find out!"

Week 23: Focused Sentences

* **Quotation Marks Before and After a Speaker's Words**

  Grandpa fixed your bike, Mom said.

* **Quotation Marks Before and After a Speaker's Words**

  Thank you, Gramps! I cried.

* **Quotation Marks Before and After a Speaker's Words**

  The back tire was bent, explained Grandpa.

* **Quotation Marks Before and After a Speaker's Words**

  I hugged him and said, You're the best!

* **Quotation Marks Before and After a Speaker's Words**

  Take it for a ride, Grandpa said.

Week 23: Corrected Sentences

* **Quotation Marks Before and After a Speaker's Words**
"Grandpa fixed your bike," Mom said.

* **Quotation Marks Before and After a Speaker's Words**
"Thank you, Gramps!" I cried.

* **Quotation Marks Before and After a Speaker's Words**
"The back tire was bent," explained Grandpa.

* **Quotation Marks Before and After a Speaker's Words**
I hugged him and said, "You're the best!"

* **Quotation Marks Before and After a Speaker's Words**
"Take it for a ride," Grandpa said.

MUG Shot Sentences

Week 24: Focused Sentences

* **Capital Letter for a Speaker's First Word**

  Mr. Ward said, "your handwriting is neat."

* **Capital Letter for a Speaker's First Word**

  I said, "thank you!"

* **Capital Letter for a Speaker's First Word**

  "can you make a sign for our door?" he asked.

* **Capital Letter for a Speaker's First Word**

  "what should the sign say?" I asked.

* **Capital Letter for a Speaker's First Word**

  Mr. Ward answered, "welcome to our class."

Week 24: Corrected Sentences

* **Capital Letter for a Speaker's First Word**

  Mr. Ward said, "Y̶your handwriting is neat."

* **Capital Letter for a Speaker's First Word**

  I said, "T̶thank you!"

* **Capital Letter for a Speaker's First Word**

  "C̶can you make a sign for our door?" he asked.

* **Capital Letter for a Speaker's First Word**

  "W̶what should the sign say?" I asked.

* **Capital Letter for a Speaker's First Word**

  Mr. Ward answered, "W̶welcome to our class."

Week 25: Focused Sentences

* **Capital Letters for Titles of Books, Stories, Poems, . . .**

  Karen and I read stone soup together.

* **Capital Letters for Titles of Books, Stories, Poems, . . .**

  I made a poster for ira sleeps over.

* **Capital Letters for Titles of Books, Stories, Poems, . . .**

  Little house on the prairie is a great book.

* **Capital Letters for Titles of Books, Stories, Poems, . . .**

  Bryce read boxcar children last week.

* **Capital Letters for Titles of Books, Stories, Poems, . . .**

  Mrs. Perez is reading stone fox to us.

MUG Shot Sentences

Week 25: Corrected Sentences

* **Capital Letters for Titles of Books, Stories, Poems, . . .**

    Karen and I read ~~s~~tone ~~s~~oup together. [S S written above]

* **Capital Letters for Titles of Books, Stories, Poems, . . .**

    I made a poster for ~~i~~ra ~~s~~leeps ~~o~~ver. [I S O written above]

* **Capital Letters for Titles of Books, Stories, Poems, . . .**

    Little ~~h~~ouse on the ~~p~~rairie is a great book. [H P written above]

* **Capital Letters for Titles of Books, Stories, Poems, . . .**

    Bryce read ~~b~~oxcar ~~c~~hildren last week. [B C written above]

* **Capital Letters for Titles of Books, Stories, Poems, . . .**

    Mrs. Perez is reading ~~s~~tone ~~f~~ox to us. [S F written above]

MUG Shot Sentences

Week 26: Focused Sentences

* **Underlining for Titles of Books and Magazines**

  We get Appleseeds magazine at our house.

* **Underlining for Titles of Books and Magazines**

  The Little House is my favorite book.

* **Underlining for Titles of Books and Magazines**

  Did you read the book When I Get Bigger?

* **Underlining for Titles of Books and Magazines**

  My little sister loves Ladybug magazine.

* **Underlining for Titles of Books and Magazines**

  We read Highlights magazines at the library.

Week 26: Corrected Sentences

* **Underlining for Titles of Books and Magazines**

    We get <u>Appleseeds</u> magazine at our house.

* **Underlining for Titles of Books and Magazines**

    <u>The Little House</u> is my favorite book.

* **Underlining for Titles of Books and Magazines**

    Did you read the book <u>When I Get Bigger</u>?

* **Underlining for Titles of Books and Magazines**

    My little sister loves <u>Ladybug</u> magazine.

* **Underlining for Titles of Books and Magazines**

    We read <u>Highlights</u> magazines at the library.

Week 27: Focused Sentences

* **Using the Right Word**

    Kara likes to read fairy tails.

* **Using the Right Word**

    Sleeping Beauty is won of her favorites.

* **Using the Right Word**

    What is you're favorite storybook?

* **Using the Right Word**

    Joseph new Rumpelstiltskin by heart.

* **Using the Right Word**

    My too favorites are Cinderella and Aladdin.

Week 27: Corrected Sentences

* **Using the Right Word**

  Kara likes to read fairy ~~tails~~ tales.

* **Using the Right Word**

  Sleeping Beauty is ~~won~~ one of her favorites.

* **Using the Right Word**

  What is ~~you're~~ your favorite storybook?

* **Using the Right Word**

  Joseph ~~new~~ knew Rumpelstiltskin by heart.

* **Using the Right Word**

  My ~~too~~ two favorites are Cinderella and Aladdin.

MUG Shot Sentences

Week 28: Mixed-Review Sentences

Penguins

* **Capitalization, Using the Right Word**

  penguin fathers warm the eggs on there feet.

* **Apostrophe to Show Ownership, Capitalization**

  a penguins baby hatches in about 55 days.

* **Apostrophe to Make a Contraction, Using the Right Word**

  At first, the babies dont look like they're parents.

* **Capitalization, Comma Between Words in a Series**

  they are brown soft and cute.

* **Apostrophe to Show Ownership, Capitalization**

  after a year, a penguins feathers are waterproof.

Week 28: Corrected Sentences

Penguins

* **Capitalization, Using the Right Word**

    ~~p~~Penguin fathers warm the eggs on ~~there~~ their feet.

* **Apostrophe to Show Ownership, Capitalization**

    ~~a~~A penguin's baby hatches in about 55 days.

* **Apostrophe to Make a Contraction, Using the Right Word**

    At first, the babies don't look like ~~they're~~ their parents.

* **Capitalization, Comma Between Words in a Series**

    ~~t~~They are brown, soft, and cute.

* **Apostrophe to Show Ownership, Capitalization**

    ~~a~~After a year, a penguin's feathers are waterproof.

Week 29: Mixed-Review Sentences

Zebras

* **Capitalization, End Punctuation**

  zebras live in large herds in africa

* **Comma to Help Set Off a Speaker's Words, Capitalization**

  Grandpa said "baby zebras weigh about 70 pounds."

* **Quotation Marks Before and After a Speaker's Words, Capitalization**

  they are called foals, the zookeeper added.

* **Apostrophe to Show Ownership, End Punctuation**

  Each zebras stripes form a different pattern

* **Using the Right Word, End Punctuation**

  Do zebras have brown hare on their backs

MUG Shot Sentences

Week 29: Corrected Sentences

Zebras

* **Capitalization, End Punctuation**
  Zebras live in large herds in Africa.

* **Comma to Help Set Off a Speaker's Words, Capitalization**
  Grandpa said, "Baby zebras weigh about 70 pounds."

* **Quotation Marks Before and After a Speaker's Words, Capitalization**
  "They are called foals," the zookeeper added.

* **Apostrophe to Show Ownership, End Punctuation**
  Each zebra's stripes form a different pattern.

* **Using the Right Word, End Punctuation**
  Do zebras have brown hair on their backs?

Week 30: Mixed-Review Sentences

Storms

* **Capitalization, Comma Between Words in a Series**

    lightning is quick surprising and dangerous.

* **Apostrophe to Make a Contraction, End Punctuation**

    Dont play outside when you see lightning

* **Apostrophe to Make a Contraction, End Punctuation**

    Johnny's puppy doesnt like the sound of thunder

* **Capitalization, Comma Between Words in a Series**

    she whines cries and shakes until John pets her.

* **Apostrophe to Show Ownership, End Punctuation**

    Does Alicias mom love to hear rain on the roof

Week 30: Corrected Sentences

Storms

* **Capitalization, Comma Between Words in a Series**

    Lightning is quick, surprising, and dangerous.

* **Apostrophe to Make a Contraction, End Punctuation**

    Don't play outside when you see lightning.

* **Apostrophe to Make a Contraction, End Punctuation**

    Johnny's puppy doesn't like the sound of thunder.

* **Capitalization, Comma Between Words in a Series**

    She whines, cries, and shakes until John pets her.

* **Apostrophe to Show Ownership, End Punctuation**

    Does Alicia's mom love to hear rain on the roof?

MUG Shot Sentences

Week 31: Mixed-Review Sentences

Tornadoes

* **Capitalization, End Punctuation**

  a tornado can cause a lot of damage

* **Capitalization, End Punctuation**

  its funnel acts like a giant vacuum cleaner

* **Capitalization, Comma Between Words in a Series**

  tornadoes can pick up trees cars and houses!

* **Capitalization, Using the Right Word**

  it maid a flat path through Grandpa's woulds!

* **Using the Right Word, Capitalization**

  My ant saw a tornado in oklahoma.

Week 31: Corrected Sentences

Tornadoes

* **Capitalization, End Punctuation**
  A tornado can cause a lot of damage.

* **Capitalization, End Punctuation**
  Its funnel acts like a giant vacuum cleaner.

* **Capitalization, Comma Between Words in a Series**
  Tornadoes can pick up trees, cars, and houses!

* **Capitalization, Using the Right Word**
  It made a flat path through Grandpa's woods!

* **Using the Right Word, Capitalization**
  My aunt saw a tornado in Oklahoma.

MUG Shot Sentences

Week 32: Mixed-Review Sentences

Seashore

* **Apostrophe to Show Ownership, End Punctuation**

   A hermit crabs body is four inches long

* **Apostrophe to Show Ownership, End Punctuation**

   Can a lizards tail be longer than its body

* **Capitalization, End Punctuation**

   oystercatcher birds live on the shores of england

* **Apostrophe to Show Ownership, End Punctuation**

   Is an oystercatchers bill wedge shaped

* **Underlining Titles, Capitalization**

   read The seashore to learn about oceans.

Week 32: Corrected Sentences

Seashore

* **Apostrophe to Show Ownership, End Punctuation**

  A hermit crab's body is four inches long.

* **Apostrophe to Show Ownership, End Punctuation**

  Can a lizard's tail be longer than its body?

* **Capitalization, End Punctuation**

  Oystercatcher birds live on the shores of England.

* **Apostrophe to Show Ownership, End Punctuation**

  Is an oystercatcher's bill wedge shaped?

* **Underlining Titles, Capitalization**

  Read <u>The Seashore</u> to learn about oceans.

Week 33: Mixed-Review Sentences

Frogs

✱ **End Punctuation, Comma Between Words in a Series**

Dear Kevin,

I'm sending you a picture of my new pet frog He is so cool His name is Fido, and he's a leopard frog I feed him worms spiders and bugs

Write back soon

                      Your friend,

                      Robby

Week 33: Corrected Sentences

Frogs

* End Punctuation, Comma Between Words in a Series

Dear Kevin,

　　I'm sending you a picture of my new pet frog. He is so cool! His name is Fido, and he's a leopard frog. I feed him worms, spiders, and bugs.

　　Write back soon.

　　　　　　　　Your friend,

　　　　　　　　Robby

Week 34: Mixed-Review Sentences

Caves

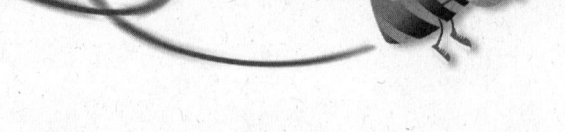

* **Comma After the Greeting and Closing in a Letter, Capitalization**

Dear robby

We're in kentucky! Yesterday we explored mammoth cave. the cave was cool, dark, and spooky. mom and emily didn't like the beetles. i thought they were neat. did you know that eyeless fish and blind insects live in the cave?

Your friend

Kevin

Week 34: Corrected Sentences

Caves

* **Comma After the Greeting and Closing in a Letter, Capitalization**

Dear Robby,

We're in Kentucky! Yesterday we explored Mammoth Cave. The cave was cool, dark, and spooky. Mom and Emily didn't like the beetles. I thought they were neat. Did you know that eyeless fish and blind insects live in the cave?

Your friend,

Kevin

Week 35: Mixed-Review Sentences

Tunnels

* **Comma to Help Set Off a Speaker's Words, Capitalization**

  I asked "do tunnels scare you, Mrs. Evans?"

* **Using the Right Word, End Punctuation**

  Tunnels go through mountains and under sees

* **Comma Between Words in a Series, Using the Right Word**

  Earthworms moles and aunts make tunnels.

* **Period After an Abbreviation, End Punctuation**

  Mr Mill asked, "Where is Windsor Tunnel"

* **Quotation Marks Before and After a Speaker's Words, Capitalization**

  Juan yelled, wow, we drove under the river!

Week 35: Corrected Sentences

Tunnels

* **Comma to Help Set Off a Speaker's Words, Capitalization**

    I asked, "do tunnels scare you, Mrs. Evans?"
    (insert comma after "asked"; capitalize D in "do")

* **Using the Right Word, End Punctuation**

    Tunnels go through mountains and under ~~sees~~ seas.

* **Comma Between Words in a Series, Using the Right Word**

    Earthworms, moles, and ~~aunts~~ ants make tunnels.

* **Period After an Abbreviation, End Punctuation**

    Mr. Mill asked, "Where is Windsor Tunnel?"

* **Quotation Marks Before and After a Speaker's Words, Capitalization**

    Juan yelled, "Wow, we drove under the river!"

MUG Shot Sentences

Week 36: Mixed-Review Sentences

Mammals

* **Capitalization, End Punctuation**

    In All About mammals we read about whales

* **Capitalization, Comma Between the Day and the Year**

    We went to the national zoo on june 18 2010.

* **Comma Between Words in a Series, End Punctuation**

    Why aren't the gorillas lions and bears more active

* **Apostrophe to Make a Contraction, End Punctuation**

    When its hot, big mammals rest a lot

* **Capitalization, Period After an Abbreviation**

    "In october, the lions are playful," said Dr Sym.

Week 36: Corrected Sentences

Mammals

* **Capitalization, End Punctuation**

  In <u>All About mammals</u> we read about whales

  (M above mammals; period added after whales)

* **Capitalization, Comma Between the Day and the Year**

  We went to the national zoo on June 18, 2010.

  (N above national; Z above zoo; J above june; comma inserted between 18 and 2010)

* **Comma Between Words in a Series, End Punctuation**

  Why aren't the gorillas, lions, and bears more active?

  (commas inserted after gorillas and lions; ? replaces .)

* **Apostrophe to Make a Contraction, End Punctuation**

  When it's hot, big mammals rest a lot.

  (apostrophe inserted in it's; period added after lot)

* **Capitalization, Period After an Abbreviation**

  "In October, the lions are playful," said Dr. Sym.

  (O above october; periods added after Dr and Sym)

© Houghton Mifflin Harcourt Publishing Company

MUG Shot Sentences

MUG Shot Paragraphs

The MUG Shot paragraphs are a quick and efficient way to review **m**echanics, **u**sage, and **g**rammar errors each week. These paragraphs also serve as proofreading exercises. Each paragraph can be corrected and discussed in 8 to 10 minutes.

Implementation and Evaluation	78
Focused Paragraphs	79
Mixed-Review Paragraphs	106

Implementation and Evaluation

For each set of MUG Shot sentences, there is a corresponding MUG Shot paragraph. The first 27 weeks of MUG Shot paragraphs focus on the same skills addressed in the sentences. The remaining 9 weeks of paragraphs feature a mixed review of proofreading and editing skills.

Implementation

A MUG Shot paragraph can be implemented at the end of the week as a review, or as an evaluation. This can be done orally as a whole-class activity. Otherwise, you may choose to distribute copies of the week's paragraph, read it aloud, and then have students make their own corrections. Afterward, go over the paragraph as a class to make sure that everyone knows what the changes are and why they are necessary. (You may want to refer to the corresponding MUG Shot sentences during your discussion.)

Evaluation

If you use the paragraphs as an evaluation activity, we recommend that you give students a basic performance score for their work. This score should reflect the number of changes the student has marked correctly (before or after any discussion). The weekly score might also reflect the student's work on the corresponding MUG Shot sentences.

MUG Shot Paragraphs

Week 1: Not Very Berry Pancakes

✱ Period at the End of a Telling Sentence

I like to cook with my dad We make blueberry pancakes The blueberries go in last One time, the batter was all ready, but we didn't have any berries We used pecans instead

Week 1: Corrected Paragraph

I like to cook with my dad⊙ We make blueberry pancakes⊙ The blueberries go in last⊙ One time, the batter was all ready, but we didn't have any berries⊙ We used pecans instead⊙

MUG Shot Paragraphs

Week 2: Flu Bug

✱ Period After an Abbreviation

    Mom took Ben to see Dr Adams. But Dr. Adams was sick! Dr. Weber was there instead. The nurse, Ms Santos, looked at Ben first. "Hmm," she said. "Ben, I think you have the flu, just like Dr Adams. I will write a note to your principal, Mrs Martinez."

Week 2: Corrected Paragraph

    Mom took Ben to see Dr. Adams. But Dr. Adams was sick! Dr. Weber was there instead. The nurse, Ms. Santos, looked at Ben first. "Hmm," she said. "Ben, I think you have the flu, just like Dr. Adams. I will write a note to your principal, Mrs. Martinez."

Week 3: Circus Man

* Period After an Initial

My great-grandpa was J Edgar Freeman. He told me about a famous circus man, P T Barnum. His circus was called "The Greatest Show on Earth." Barnum and his friend, James A Bailey, formed a new circus. It became the "Ringling Bros. and Barnum & Bailey Circus." It still visits many towns each year.

Week 3: Corrected Paragraph

My great-grandpa was J. Edgar Freeman. He told me about a famous circus man, P. T. Barnum. His circus was called "The Greatest Show on Earth." Barnum and his friend, James A. Bailey, formed a new circus. It became the "Ringling Bros. and Barnum & Bailey Circus." It still visits many towns each year.

Week 4: The State of Things

* **Question Mark After a Question**

    Jake asked lots of questions about the United States: How many states are there What state do we live in What is the biggest state What is the smallest state Can we go visit another state

Week 4: Corrected Paragraph

    Jake asked lots of questions about the United States: How many states are there? What state do we live in? What is the biggest state? What is the smallest state? Can we go visit another state?

Week 5: Home Run!

* **Exclamation Point After a Sentence That Shows Strong Feeling**

    Oh no, Max struck out Our best batter is up next. Gloria is our last hope. She swings and misses Here comes the next pitch. She smacks it over the fence

Week 5: Corrected Paragraph

    Oh no, Max struck out! Our best batter is up next. Gloria is our last hope. She swings and misses! Here comes the next pitch. She smacks it over the fence!

Week 6: Write Soon!

✱ Capital Letter for the First Word in a Sentence

i love getting letters in the mail. when Grandmom and Grandpop Dodd go on trips, they send me postcards when they go on trips. grandpa Charlie sent me some bean seeds to plant. sometimes Aunt Suzanne sends me funny poems, jokes, and pictures. I write back to all of them.

Week 6: Corrected Paragraph

i love getting letters in the mail. when Grandmom and Grandpop Dodd go on trips, they send me postcards when they go on trips. grandpa Charlie sent me some bean seeds to plant. sometimes Aunt Suzanne sends me funny poems, jokes, and pictures. I write back to all of them.

MUG Shot Paragraphs

Week 7: Bad Start Poem

* **Capital Letter for the Word "I"**

    i had a bad start today.

    i missed the bus,

    i was late for school,

    and i didn't get to play.

    The next time things start off that way,

    i think i'll go back to bed all day.

Week 7: Corrected Poem

    i̸ had a bad start today.

    i̸ missed the bus,

    i̸ was late for school,

    and i̸ didn't get to play.

    The next time things start off that way,

    i̸ think i̸'ll go back to bed all day.

Week 8: Party Time

✱ **Capital Letters for Days, Months, and Holidays**

On monday, we planned some class parties. First we'll have a valentine's day party. It will be on the second friday in February. The next friday will be our presidents' day party. In april we'll have an earth day party.

Week 8: Corrected Paragraph

On ^M^monday, we planned some class parties. First we'll have a ^V^valentine's ^D^day party. It will be on the second ^F^friday in February. The next ^F^friday will be our ^P^presidents' ^D^day party. In ^A^april we'll have an ^E^earth ^D^day party.

Week 9: Places to Go

* Capital Letters for Names of Places

Our class made a graph of places we'd like to visit. Most people voted for florida. Others wanted to see the statue of liberty. Some people voted for yellowstone national park. Some wanted to see the atlantic ocean or the pacific ocean.

Week 9: Corrected Paragraph

Our class made a graph of places we'd like to visit. Most people voted for **F**lorida. Others wanted to see the **S**tatue of **L**iberty. Some people voted for **Y**ellowstone **N**ational **P**ark. Some wanted to see the **A**tlantic **O**cean or the **P**acific **O**cean.

MUG Shot Paragraphs

Week 10: What a Throw!

* **Capital Letters for Names and Titles**

John price and carlos torres played catch. Their ball went into mr. stone's garden. Carlos knocked, and mrs. stone came to the door. "I'll get your ball, carlos," she said. She threw it over the fence to him. Mrs. stone can really throw!

Week 10: Corrected Paragraph

John ~~p~~**P**rice and ~~c~~**C**arlos ~~t~~**T**orres played catch. Their ball went into ~~m~~**M**r. ~~s~~**S**tone's garden. Carlos knocked, and ~~m~~**M**rs. ~~s~~**S**tone came to the door. "I'll get your ball, ~~c~~**C**arlos," she said. She threw it over the fence to him. Mrs. ~~s~~**S**tone can really throw!

MUG Shot Paragraphs

Week 11: Crazy Picnic

✱ Plurals That Add "es"

The foxs and ostrichs had a crazy picnic. First, they played a word game. The foxs made guesss, and the ostrichs had hunchs. The foxs won, but the ostrichs didn't mind. They all ate sack lunchs and made huge messs. They swam in a pond and made big, muddy splashs. Then they got into two buss and headed home.

Week 11: Corrected Paragraph

The ~~foxs~~ (foxes) and ~~ostrichs~~ (ostriches) had a crazy picnic. First, they played a word game. The ~~foxs~~ (foxes) made ~~guesss~~ (guesses), and the ~~ostrichs~~ (ostriches) had ~~hunchs~~ (hunches). The ~~foxs~~ (foxes) won, but the ~~ostrichs~~ (ostriches) didn't mind. They all ate sack ~~lunchs~~ (lunches) and made huge ~~messs~~ (messes). They swam in a pond and made big, muddy ~~splashs~~ (splashes). Then they got into two ~~buss~~ (buses) and headed home.

MUG Shot Paragraphs

Week 12: Sharing a Book

* **Using the Right Word**

Deer Sofia,

Eye read a good book. It's called <u>Rosie's Birthday Rat</u>. I'll bring it to school four you. I no your going to like it, to.

You're friend,

Mariel

Week 12: Corrected Paragraph

~~Deer~~ **Dear** Sofia,

~~Eye~~ **I** read a good book. It's called <u>Rosie's Birthday Rat</u>. I'll bring it to school ~~four~~ **for** you. I ~~no~~ ~~your~~ **know you're** going to like it, ~~to~~ **too**.

~~You're~~ **Your** friend,

Mariel

Week 13: Where, Oh Where?

* **Comma Between a City and a State**

There's a Lincoln Nebraska, and a Lincoln Illinois. There's a Jackson Mississippi, and a Jackson Wyoming. There's a Columbus Ohio, and a Columbus Wisconsin. There's an Austin Texas, and an Austin Minnesota. All these cities were named after people.

Week 13: Corrected Paragraph

There's a Lincoln, Nebraska, and a Lincoln, Illinois. There's a Jackson, Mississippi, and a Jackson, Wyoming. There's a Columbus, Ohio, and a Columbus, Wisconsin. There's an Austin, Texas, and an Austin, Minnesota. All these cities were named after people.

MUG Shot Paragraphs

Week 14: 225 Birthdays

✱ Comma Between the Day and the Year

On July 4 1776, the Declaration of Independence was signed. That was the day the United States was born. The United States was 100 on July 4 1876, and 200 on July 4 1976. July 4 2001, was our country's 225th birthday.

Week 14: Corrected Paragraph

On July 4, 1776, the Declaration of Independence was signed. That was the day the United States was born. The United States was 100 on July 4, 1876, and 200 on July 4, 1976. July 4, 2001, was our country's 225th birthday.

Week 15: Tea Party

* **Comma After the Greeting and the Closing in a Letter**

Dear Kathryn

    Yes! I would love to come to your tea party. May I bring my kitty? She will skip her catnap if you rub her ears.

                          Love

                          Grandma Diane

Week 15: Corrected Paragraph

Dear Kathryn,

    Yes! I would love to come to your tea party. May I bring my kitty? She will skip her catnap if you rub her ears.

                          Love,

                        Grandma Diane

Week 16: The Teacher's Story

✱ Using the Right Word

    My teacher's camping trip turned into quite a tail. First, aunts got into her food. Then a bare eight the food, ants and all. Next, a storm blue down her tent, and the rain got her would wet. "I didn't no camping would be sew exciting!" she said.

Week 16: Corrected Paragraph

    My teacher's camping trip turned into quite a ~~tail~~ *tale*. First, ~~aunts~~ *ants* got into her food. Then a ~~bare eight~~ *bear ate* the food, ants and all. Next, a storm ~~blue~~ *blew* down her tent, and the rain got her ~~would~~ *wood* wet. "I didn't ~~no~~ *know* camping would be ~~sew~~ *so* exciting!" she said.

Week 17: Waiting for Willie

✱ Apostrophe to Make a Contraction

I havent finished my painting. Willie hasnt finished his, either. I cant finish until hes done with the yellow paint. Last week he didnt finish until after the bell rang. Im afraid I wont get to finish.

Week 17: Corrected Paragraph

I haven't finished my painting. Willie hasn't finished his, either. I can't finish until he's done with the yellow paint. Last week he didn't finish until after the bell rang. I'm afraid I won't get to finish.

Week 18: Camping

✱ Apostrophe to Show Ownership

The moons glow gave us light.

A dogs howl sang through the night.

Our tents door was shut tight.

But a cats yowl still gave us a fright.

Week 18: Corrected Paragraph

The moon's glow gave us light.

A dog's howl sang through the night.

Our tent's door was shut tight.

But a cat's yowl still gave us a fright.

Week 19: The Goose Parade

✱ Irregular Plurals

Today, I saw a mother goose leading her babys to the river. The gooses had to cross a very busy street. Two womans stopped traffic so the goose family could cross safely. The gooses walked across the muddy riverbank. Their foots left prints in the mud.

Week 19: Corrected Paragraph

Today, I saw a mother goose leading her ~~babys~~ **babies** to the river. The ~~gooses~~ **geese** had to cross a very busy street. Two ~~womans~~ **women** stopped traffic so the goose family could cross safely. The ~~gooses~~ **geese** walked across the muddy riverbank. Their ~~foots~~ **feet** left prints in the mud.

Week 20: Aloha

* **Comma Between Words in a Series**

    Hawaii is warm sunny and beautiful. Farmers grow sugarcane pineapples and coffee. Insects snails birds and bats were once the only animals there. People brought dogs cats pigs and many other animals.

Week 20: Corrected Paragraph

    Hawaii is warm, sunny, and beautiful. Farmers grow sugarcane, pineapples, and coffee. Insects, snails, birds, and bats were once the only animals there. People brought dogs, cats, pigs, and many other animals.

Week 21: Choices

* Comma in Compound Sentences

When I stand in the lunch line, I must make choices. I can have a hot lunch or I can choose a cold sandwich. Usually, I bring my lunch to school but today I didn't. I think I will choose a hot lunch and I will eat with my friend Sarika.

Week 21: Corrected Paragraph

When I stand in the lunch line, I must make choices. I can have a hot lunch, or I can choose a cold sandwich. Usually, I bring my lunch to school, but today I didn't. I think I will choose a hot lunch, and I will eat with my friend Sarika.

Week 22: Treats for All

✱ Comma to Help Set Off a Speaker's Words

Mrs. Tran said "Michael and Kamila, you can get your treat now. Everyone, Michael brought a treat for the class." Michael and Kamila came back with two giant boxes.

"Wow! That's a lot of apples" Suzie said.

"My mom works at an orchard" Michael explained.

Week 22: Corrected Paragraph

Mrs. Tran said, "Michael and Kamila, you can get your treat now. Everyone, Michael brought a treat for the class." Michael and Kamila came back with two giant boxes.

"Wow! That's a lot of apples," Suzie said.

"My mom works at an orchard," Michael explained.

Week 23: Cold Feet

* **Quotation Marks Before and After a Speaker's Words**

    Grandpa asked, Will you sing for us, or do you have cold feet?

    My feet aren't cold. I'm just scared, I said.

    It's a saying, Grandpa said. Cold feet means to be afraid to do something.

    Oh, I said. Well, I guess my feet are frozen!

Week 23: Corrected Paragraph

    Grandpa asked, "Will you sing for us, or do you have cold feet?"

    "My feet aren't cold. I'm just scared," I said.

    "It's a saying," Grandpa said. "Cold feet means to be afraid to do something."

    "Oh," I said. "Well, I guess my feet are frozen!"

Week 24: A New Leaf

✲ **Capital Letter for a Speaker's First Word**

Mom said, "i'm going to turn over a new leaf."

I asked, "what do you mean?"

"i'm going to walk two miles every day," she said.

I asked, "what does that have to do with turning over a leaf?"

"It means changing for the better," she said.

Week 24: Corrected Paragraph

Mom said, "*I*'m going to turn over a new leaf."

I asked, "*W*hat do you mean?"

"*I*'m going to walk two miles every day," she said.

I asked, "*W*hat does that have to do with turning over a leaf?"

"It means changing for the better," she said.

Week 25: From Page to Stage

* **Capital Letters for Titles of Books, Stories, Poems . . .**

We all performed poems this week. My group performed "hurt no living thing." Another group performed "something told the wild geese." My favorite was "old crocodile." We are going to put all the poems in a book. It will be called great performances.

Week 25: Corrected Paragraph

We all performed poems this week. My group performed "**H**urt **N**o **L**iving **T**hing." Another group performed "**S**omething **T**old the **W**ild **G**eese." My favorite was "**O**ld **C**rocodile." We are going to put all the poems in a book. It will be called **G**reat **P**erformances.

Week 26: Arthur and Clifford

* **Underlining for Titles of Books and Magazines**

Melanie likes books about Arthur. Her favorites are Arthur's April Fool and Arthur's Teacher Trouble. I like books about Clifford. My favorites are Clifford and the Grouchy Neighbors and Clifford's Sports Day. Melanie and I both like to read stories in Spider magazine.

Week 26: Corrected Paragraph

Melanie likes books about Arthur. Her favorites are <u>Arthur's April Fool</u> and <u>Arthur's Teacher Trouble</u>. I like books about Clifford. My favorites are <u>Clifford and the Grouchy Neighbors</u> and <u>Clifford's Sports Day</u>. Melanie and I both like to read stories in <u>Spider</u> magazine.

Week 27: Best Dressed

✸ Using the Right Word

    You should sea the outfit Carla maid for the class play. Her neighbor helped her so it. She will where it tonight. I no her costume will be the best won.

Week 27: Corrected Paragraph

    You should ~~sea~~ *see* the outfit Carla ~~maid~~ *made* for the class play. Her neighbor helped her ~~so~~ *sew* it. She will ~~where~~ *wear* it tonight. I ~~no~~ *know* her costume will be the best ~~won~~ *one*.

MUG Shot Paragraphs

Week 28: Keep Moving

✱ **Capitalization, Apostrophe to Make a Contraction**

most penguins live in antarctica. a penguin's fat keeps it warm. although penguins cant fly, theyre good swimmers. they also slide on their bellies. they use their wings and feet to push along.

Week 28: Corrected Paragraph

~~m~~Most penguins live in ~~a~~Antarctica. ~~a~~A penguin's fat keeps it warm. ~~a~~Although penguins can't fly, they're good swimmers. ~~t~~They also slide on their bellies. ~~t~~They use their wings and feet to push along.

Week 29: Show Your Stripes

✱ Quotation Marks Before and After a Speaker's Words, End Punctuation

I asked, Are all zebras black and white

Some zebras have some brown hair, the zookeeper said Some zebras are light yellow and black

Grandpa asked, Do many zebras live in the wild

The zookeeper answered, One kind of zebra is already extinct Another kind is nearly gone, too.

Week 29: Corrected Paragraph

I asked, "Are all zebras black and white?"

"Some zebras have some brown hair," the zookeeper said. "Some zebras are light yellow and black."

Grandpa asked, "Do many zebras live in the wild?"

The zookeeper answered, "One kind of zebra is already extinct. Another kind is nearly gone, too."

Week 30: No Fireworks, Please

✱ Capitalization, Apostrophe to Make a Contraction

some people like thunderstorms, but others dont. jerry's dad says theyre fun to watch. he says lightning's bright flashes are like free fireworks. jerry's little brother says he doesnt like thunderstorms or noisy fireworks.

Week 30: Corrected Paragraph

$\overset{S}{\cancel{s}}$ome people like thunderstorms, but others don$\overset{,}{\cancel{\,}}$t. $\overset{J}{\cancel{j}}$erry's dad says they$\overset{,}{\,}$re fun to watch. $\overset{H}{\cancel{h}}$e says lightning's bright flashes are like free fireworks. $\overset{J}{\cancel{j}}$erry's little brother says he doesn$\overset{,}{\,}$t like thunderstorms or noisy fireworks.

Week 31: Funnel Clouds

* **Capitalization, Comma Between Words in a Series**

tornadoes are huge loud and scary. they are common in texas oklahoma and other southern states. do you know how to stay safe during a tornado? if not, ask a teacher police officer or firefighter what to do.

Week 31: Corrected Paragraph

Tornadoes are huge, loud, and scary. They are common in Texas, Oklahoma, and other southern states. Do you know how to stay safe during a tornado? If not, ask a teacher, police officer, or firefighter what to do.

MUG Shot Paragraphs

Week 32: Ahoy, Captain

✱ Apostrophe to Show Ownership, End Punctuation

Terrys grandparents went to the seashore They brought him a captains cap Terry thanked them for the great cap. Then he asked them, "Where is my boat" That question made Terrys grandpa laugh

Week 32: Corrected Paragraph

Terry's grandparents went to the seashore. They brought him a captain's cap. Terry thanked them for the great cap. Then he asked them, "Where is my boat?" That question made Terry's grandpa laugh.

Week 33: Fido the Frog

✱ End Punctuation, Comma Between Words in a Series

Dear Robby,

    You're right Fido is cool I have seen toads bullfrogs and spring peepers Fido is the first leopard frog I've seen How old is he How big will he get

                       Your pal,

                       Kevin

Week 33: Corrected Paragraph

Dear Robby,

    You're right. Fido is cool. I have seen toads, bullfrogs, and spring peepers. Fido is the first leopard frog I've seen. How old is he? How big will he get?

                       Your pal,

                       Kevin

Week 34: Cave Stories

✱ **Comma After the Greeting and Closing in a Letter, Capitalization**

Dear kevin

Your trip to Mammoth cave, kentucky, sounds awesome. dad read me a book called tom sawyer. tom gets lost in a big cave. it is scary! write soon.

                        Your friend

                        robby

Week 34: Corrected Paragraph

Dear ~~k~~Kevin**,**

    Your trip to Mammoth ~~c~~Cave, ~~k~~Kentucky, sounds awesome. ~~d~~Dad read me a book called ~~t~~Tom ~~s~~Sawyer. ~~t~~Tom gets lost in a big cave. ~~i~~It is scary! ~~w~~Write soon.

                        Your friend**,**
                        ~~r~~Robby

Week 35: Tunnel Trouble

✱ **Comma to Set Off a Speaker's Words, Period After an Abbreviation**

"Mrs Evans, do tunnels scare you?" I asked.

"Of course not " Mrs Evans answered.

Then Mr Evans spoke up. He said "Mrs Evans is forgetting that tunnel in Colorado."

"Oh, that tunnel *was* scary " Mrs Evans said.

Week 35: Corrected Paragraph

"Mrs. Evans, do tunnels scare you?" I asked.

"Of course not," Mrs. Evans answered.

Then Mr. Evans spoke up. He said, "Mrs. Evans is forgetting that tunnel in Colorado."

"Oh, that tunnel *was* scary," Mrs. Evans said.

Week 36: Bears

✱ **Capitalization, Comma Between Words in a Series**

   We went to the national zoo in june. We were there on a tuesday, so it wasn't too crowded. Our favorite animals were the monkeys giraffes and bears. The baby bears played swam and ate fruit.

Week 36: Corrected Paragraph

   We went to the *N*ational *Z*oo in *J*une. We were there on a *T*uesday, so it wasn't too crowded. Our favorite animals were the monkeys, giraffes, and bears. The baby bears played, swam, and ate fruit.

Daily Writing Practice

This section offers three types of writing practice. The freewriting done in response to the **writing prompts** can be shared in follow-up sessions and later shaped into finished writing. The discussion of daily journal writing introduces lists of **writing topics**. The topics address a wide range of writing ideas. Finally, "showing" in writing, developed by expanding on the **Show-Me sentences**, can be shared in follow-up sessions and later shaped into finished descriptive paragraphs.

Writing Prompts	**116**
Writing Topics	**141**
Show-Me Sentences	**145**

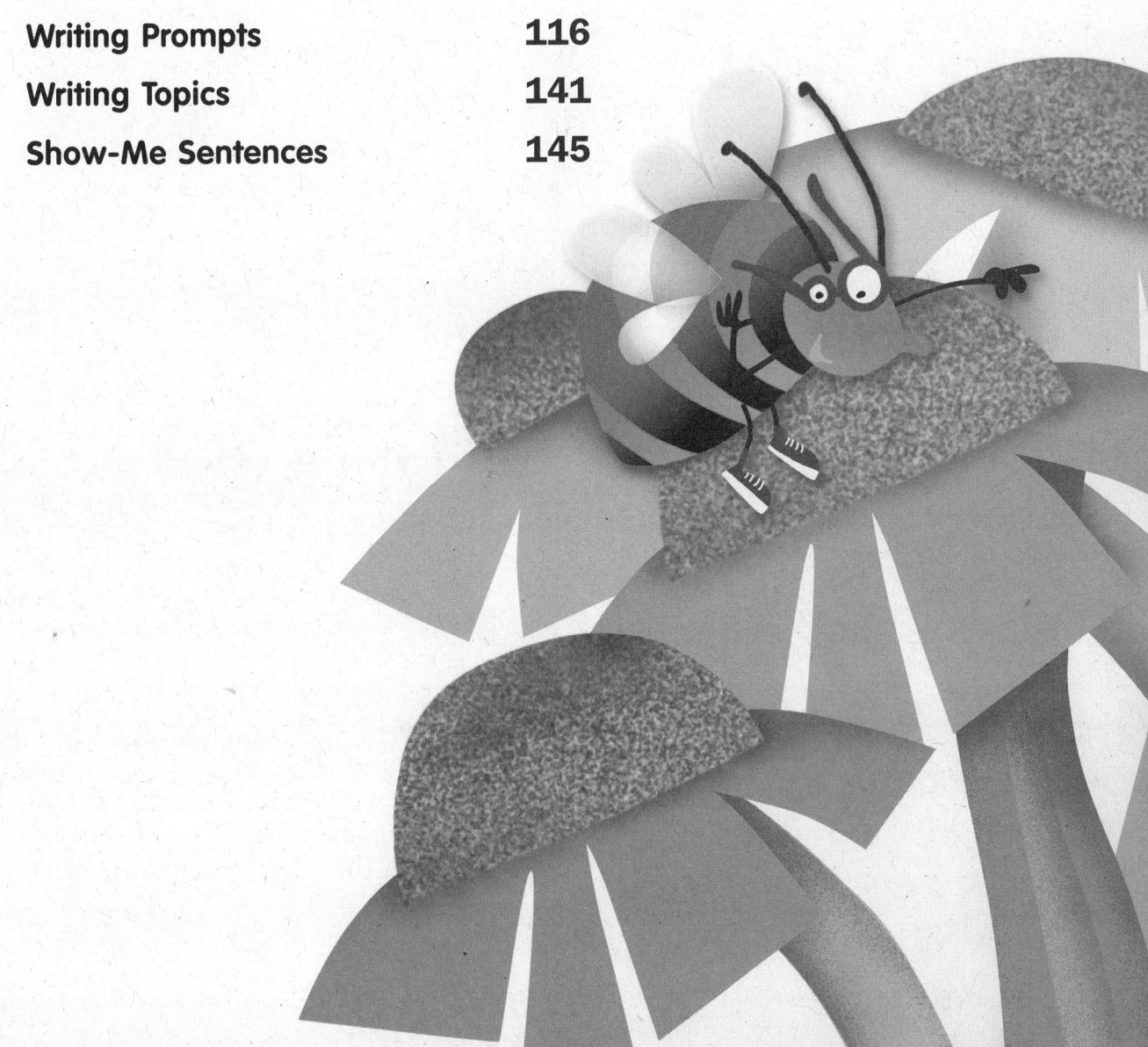

Writing Prompts

Introducing Writing Prompts

Remind students that they can become better writers by practicing every day. Writing in journals and diaries is one way to do this. Sometimes it helps to have a starting point for daily writing. These writing starters are often called writing prompts.

Forms of Writing Prompts

Writing prompts use a variety of starting points.

Pictures Pictures can remind students of something they have seen or done or a place they have been. Talking about a picture or allowing students to talk briefly with a partner will help them get started.

Possible Titles Discuss some of the different ideas evoked by the same title. This demonstrates the students' freedom to take off in their own directions.

Sentence Starters Introduce sentence starters by doing some orally in class. Stress that there are no right answers. If students have several good ideas, tell them that they may want to keep track of these for later writing practice.

Questions A question naturally prompts a written response. Questions may also serve as possible titles.

Note: Remember that the purpose of a prompt is to get the flow of words started. The finished writing may be quite removed from the original prompt. (If you wish to have students respond specifically to a prompt, make that clear to them.)

Think and Write

First, have students look at the writing prompt and think about it. As soon as they get an idea, they should start writing. Have them keep writing until they run out of ideas or come to the end of their stories.

Time to Stop!

You may ask students to write for a certain amount of time. It may be helpful to tell them when the time is nearly over.

Share

Students often enjoy sharing their writing with one another. Set aside time for students to read their writing to a partner or the class. Sharing writing soon after it is finished, while it is still fresh in their minds, may be the best plan for young writers. Have students color the pictures on the writing prompt pages for a bulletin board display.

Save Your Writing

Writing prompts may give students good story ideas, or start them thinking about other topics they would like to write about. Set up a place for students to save their writing so they can come back to it later.

WRITING PROMPT

I couldn't believe my eyes.

WRITING PROMPT

The Trick I Played

WRITING PROMPT

Why do I like trees?

WRITING PROMPT

How did I learn to ride a bike?

WRITING PROMPT

The turtle had to hurry.

WRITING PROMPT

A storm is coming.

WRITING PROMPT

Which faraway place would I like to visit?

WRITING PROMPT

Things I Like to Think About

WRITING PROMPT

Who should get an award?

WRITING PROMPT

I was so sick.

WRITING PROMPT

Mom's or Dad's Craziest Idea

WRITING PROMPT

When I grow up . . .

WRITING PROMPT

It was hilarious.

WRITING PROMPT

I peeked into the hole.

WRITING PROMPT

What if I could drive a car?

WRITING PROMPT

I'd like to take a ride on . . .

WRITING PROMPT

If I Could Touch a Rainbow

WRITING PROMPT

I Didn't Mean To

WRITING PROMPT

I felt good when I helped . . .

WRITING PROMPT

The Monster Cave

WRITING PROMPT

My Best Idea

WRITING PROMPT

My Time Machine

WRITING PROMPT

I wish I could . . .

WRITING PROMPT

My Favorite Place

Writing Topics
Writing Topics and Daily Journal Writing

> "I can tap into [my students'] human instinct to write if I help them realize that their lives and memories are worth telling stories about, and if I help them zoom in on topics of fundamental importance to them."
>
> —writing teacher JUNE GOULD

As classroom teachers, we know from experience that the personal stories young learners love to share can serve as the basis of an effective and lively writing program. Here's how we did it.

Getting Started

At the beginning of the school year, we introduced in-class journal writing to the students. We knew that the most effective way to get students into writing was simply to let them write often and freely about their own lives, without having to worry about grades or turning their writing in. This helped them develop a feel for "real" writing—writing that comes from their own thoughts and feelings.

That's where the journals come in. Nothing gets students into writing more effectively than a personal journal. (And no other type of writing is so easy to implement.) All your students need are spiral notebooks, pencils, time to write, and encouragement to explore whatever is on their minds.

We provided our students with four or five personal writing topics each time they wrote. They could use one of these topics as a starting point, or write about something else entirely. The choice was theirs.

Writing Topics

To start off an exercise, we posted suggested writing topics like these:

- your most memorable kitchen-related experience,
- your favorite time of the day,
- coping with brothers or sisters,
- the day of the big storm, or
- what you did over the weekend.

Students would either choose from the list or write on a topic they preferred. See pages 142–144 in this book for more suggested topics. We asked our students to write every other day for the first 5–10 minutes of the class period. (Every Monday, Wednesday, and Friday were writing days.) Of course, we had to adjust our schedule at times, but, for the most part, the students wrote three times a week.

Keep It Going

After everyone was seated and roll was taken, the journals were passed out, the topics were given, and everyone wrote. We expected students to write for a full 5–10 minutes, nonstop. They knew that they would earn a quarterly grade based on their participation in the journal writing.

Daily Writing Practice

Writing Topics

Birthdays
My favorite birthday celebration
Birthday games
A great present
The best gift I ever gave
Recipe for a fun birthday
Summer birthdays
Winter birthdays
A birthday surprise
A birthday adventure

Holidays
Our family celebrates . . .
A holiday meal
A special holiday tradition
My favorite holiday
A holiday that didn't work out as planned
A holiday game
Parades
School parties
Thanksgiving
Veteran's Day
The Fourth of July fireworks

My Neighborhood
My closest neighbors
Our grocery store
Trees near my house
Birds that live near my house
Wild animals in my area
Transportation in my neighborhood
I can walk to . . .
From my home, I can see . . .
A park I visit
My school

Community Helpers
The crossing guard
My school bus driver
The librarian
School principal
Lifeguards
Firefighters
Street department workers
Favorite clerks
Teacher's aide
Summer recreation director
Camp counselor
Coaches

Daily Writing Practice

Mammals

The strangest animal in the zoo
An animal family reunion
Unusual animal homes
Animals I'd like to see in the wild
Compare two animals
How are some animals like people?
How are some people like animals?
If _____ could talk
Farm animals

Feelings

When I lose a tooth, . . .
One thing I worry about
Something that makes me smile
Sometimes I frown when . . .
I'm happy when . . .
I look forward to . . .
I get scared if . . .
I feel bored if . . .
It's exciting when . . .
I don't like to feel . . .
I always feel better when . . .
I felt brave when . . .

Friends

A new classmate
A new neighbor
Animal friends
Pen pals
Moving to a new place
Making something with a friend
Friends who move away
Sleepovers
Baking a treat together
Recess times
Sports teams
My teacher

Transportation

Traveling by train
Why I like (don't like) flying
Going by bus
Taking a taxicab
My favorite boat ride
Biking adventures
Skateboards and scooters
Snowboards
My first motorcycle ride
Skis
In-line skating
Rollercoaster rides
Canoeing
Carnival rides
Sailing
A horse-and-buggy ride
Horseback riding

Daily Writing Practice

Nutrition

My favorite fruits
A healthful meal
How to set the table
Recipe for a healthful snack
A complete breakfast
Packing a picnic
My worst food experience
In my vegetable garden
Food in the news
Foods I don't like
Lunchtime food trading
Cooking adventures

Communication

Sign language
Writing notes for fun
The family bulletin board
Answering machine messages
E-mail buddies
Recording voice-mail greetings
Television news
Newspaper headlines
Internet
Longhand letters
Cell phones
Pager police
Fax machines

Book Characters

Frog and Toad
Arthur
Nate the Great
Amelia Bedelia
Junie B. Jones
Your choice _____

Fairy-Tale Characters

Gingerbread Man
Three Billy Goats Gruff
Little Red Hen
Goldilocks and the Three Bears
Hansel and Gretel
Rumpelstiltskin
Rapunzel
Snow White and the Seven Dwarfs
Beauty and the Beast
Your choice _____

Games

Tag
Hide-and-seek
Four square
Jump rope
Dodgeball
Fox and Goose
Softball
Basketball
HORSE
Kick ball
Soccer
Computer
Races
Puzzles

Daily Writing Practice

Show-Me Sentences
Introducing Show-Me Sentences

Teachers have always said to their students, "Your writing needs details" or "This idea is too general." We even know of a teacher who had a special stamp made: "Give more examples."

So how could this problem be approached? It's obvious that simply telling students to add more details and examples is not enough. Even showing them how professional writers develop their ideas is not enough (although this does help). Students learn to add substance and depth to their writing through regular practice.

Here's one method that has worked for many students and teachers: the Show-Me sentences. Students begin with a basic topic—"My desk is messy," for example—and create several sentences or a brief paragraph that *shows* rather than *tells*. The sentence is a springboard for lively writing.

About Show-Me Sentences . . .

The following pages contain 50 Show-Me sentences. Each sentence speaks directly to students, so they should have little difficulty creating several sentences or a short paragraph full of personal details. Again, we suggest that you use these sentences several days a week for an extended period of time (at least one month).

Note: By design, each page of Show-Me sentences can be made into an overhead transparency.

Implementation

DAY ONE Before you ask students to work on their own, develop a Show-Me sentence as a class. Write a sample sentence on the board. Have students volunteer specific details that give this basic thought some life. List their ideas on the board. Next, construct a brief paragraph on the board using some of these details. (Make no mention of the original sentence in your paragraph.) Discuss the results. Make sure that your students see how specific details help create a visual image for the reader.

DAY TWO Have students work on their first Show-Me sentences in class. Upon completion of their writing, have pairs of students share the results of their work. Then ask for volunteers to share their writing with the entire class.

Note: Reserve the first 5–10 minutes of a class period for writing or discussing.

Daily Writing Practice

Evaluation

Have students reserve a section in their notebooks for their writing, or have them compile their work in a folder. At regular intervals, give them some type of performance score (a check, for example) for their efforts. At the end of the unit, have them select one or two of their best examples to revise and then submit for a thorough evaluation.

Sample Show-Me Writing

✶ I like books.

My room is full of books. Some are really old. Others are shiny and new. I read my books over and over again. Some are like good friends. When I was little, my dad read to me. Now I can read books by myself. I still like it when my dad reads to me.

Show-Me Sentences

* My bike is dirty.

* People can have many friends at once.

* My collection keeps me busy.

* Yesterday I felt lonely.

* Our garage needs cleaning.

Show-Me Sentences

* The house was a mess.

* The game was awesome!

* Camp is fun.

* My_____ (pet) is a good friend.

* The teacher was upset.

Show-Me Sentences

* My _____ (sister, brother) got muddy.

* I like pizza.

* My schoolbag is full of stuff.

* It was dark, and I was scared.

* The sunrise was beautiful.

Show-Me Sentences

✳ There were two ducks in our yard.

✳ We "baby-sat" for our friend's dog.

✳ My family has a vegetable garden.

✳ The tree house was fun.

✳ Something on the stove smelled terrible.

Show-Me Sentences

* My closet is too full.

* I like going barefoot.

* She looked sad.

* We celebrated my uncle's birthday.

* Mom needed a rest.

Show-Me Sentences

* Autumn leaves have pretty colors.

* Today is hot and muggy.

* He tripped and fell.

* I don't like washing dishes.

* Building sand castles is fun.

Show-Me Sentences

* The sky is cloudy.

* The town was destroyed.

* I read a great book.

* Music makes me happy.

* My _____ (brother, sister) bugs me.

Show-Me Sentences

* That was a long car trip.

* It stormed last night.

* We packed for our vacation.

* Visiting my friend's house is fun.

* I was tired.

Show-Me Sentences

* My _____ (mom, dad) works hard.

* We picked up all the litter.

* Our team won the game.

* I broke my skateboard.

* It was an accident.

Show-Me Sentences

* I like to make lunch.

* Our refrigerator holds lots of things.

* Dad and I grocery shop.

* The pantry looks empty.

* The music sounded too loud.